Diesel

CUTTING EDGE

TED POLHEMUS

Diesel

World Wide Wear

WATSON-GUPTILL
PUBLICATIONS
New York

First published in 1998 in the United States of America
by Watson-Guptill Publications, a division of
BPI Communications, Inc.,
1515 Broadway, New York, NY 10036

Library of Congress Catalog Card Number: 98-86823

ISBN 0-8230-1203-4

This book was conceived,
designed, and produced by
THE IVY PRESS LTD
2/3 St Andrews Place
Lewes
East Sussex BN7 1UP

Art Director: Terry Jeavons
Design and page layout: Harry Green
Commissioning Editor: Christine Davis
Editorial Director: Sophie Collins

Printed in Hong Kong

Contents

Diesel has always operated and will always operate in an independent, instinctive manner—from the heart more than from the head. If you believe in something, you must concentrate on it. Focus. Go straight to the point. Straight on course. You must do what you like, what you believe in. This is the secret of our success here at Diesel. We do what we like, what makes us smile. We never do things just because we're supposed to do them."

Renzo Rosso

"WELCOME TO the Diesel planet." This is how they answer the telephone at Diesel Industries—makers of world-renowned anti-fashion fashion, and what are probably the world's most surreal advertisements. And what a strange planet it is. A place where here and now can be anywhere and any time. A post-modern planet that time-warps the past into the future—and the future into the past—while sampling and mixing all known (and some unknown) intergalactic cultures into a funky, cosmic mélange.

And what intelligent life forms they are, these creatures from planet Diesel. Instead of beaming down on some dreary military base in a barely habitable American desert, they have cleverly chosen to make their base of operations the rolling, pneumatic hills and medieval piazzas of the Bassano del Grappa region of northern Italy, where the quality of the local wine is exceeded only by that of the local asparagus. It is from this unlikely spot that planet Diesel's mysterious "clothing engineers" embark on "research expeditions" to some of planet Earth's most esoteric (and, more often than not, hippest) locales.

Clever, too, to disguise their interplanetary invasion as a fashion design company—thereby hiding what might otherwise be construed as strange activities, and even stranger appearances, behind a smokescreen of trendy eccentricity.

Thus, garments layered with a metallic mesh to retain a perpetually crumpled appearance seem an amusing novelty rather than the foil to Earth's airport metal detectors that they obviously are. Thus, a fake martial arts book entitled *Fight Me* (a barely coded call to arms and anarchy) gets passed off as a weird and wacky clothing catalog. Thus, a jacket printed with instructions from a U.S. tank manual is seen as radical chic rather than blatant espionage. And thus, advertisements that mock everything from American evangelism to Japanese consumerism, from Alpine village life to geriatric sun-worshippers, win awards for their wry humor rather than get condemned as sinister brainwashing.

If further proof were needed, we have only to look at the unlikely speed and extent of Diesel's success in transforming itself from a tiny Italian jeans manufacturer to an international brand name that is recognized and coveted from Moscow to Melbourne, Cape Town to Chicago. There is also to be considered the improbable nature of Diesel's director, one Renzo Rosso—the inhumanly energetic mastermind who openly admits to "looking to the stars" for his inspiration.

The Italian dream

Naturally, the official story put out by Diesel's own press office makes no mention of interplanetary space travel. What it tells us instead is that Renzo Rosso was born in 1955 near Padua,

"Welcome to the Diesel planet." The reception desk at Diesel Industry's headquarters.

Diesel on the catwalk: the fall/winter 1997 collection shown in New York.

northeast Italy, to farming parents. That he attended the local technical college, where he studied textiles and manufacturing. That through friends from Marconi he was introduced to Adriano Goldschmied, "the pioneer of Italian casualwear," who offered him a job in his Moltex company. That, in 1978, Goldschmied and Rosso together founded a company called Diesel (the name, Rosso readily points out, was conceived by Goldschmied), which Rosso then bought complete ownership of in 1985.

Renzo Rosso has long exemplified a global (if not galactic) perspective; nevertheless, his company's Italian context is all-important in understanding its development. Italy emerged from World War II with its traditions of craftsmanship in tailoring and textile manufacture intact, and it is hardly surprising that the country soon established an international reputation for well-made, elegant clothing. What is perhaps more surprising to those of us who are not Italian and who grew up longing to emulate the sartorial finesse of the likes of Marcello Mastroianni in *La Dolce Vita*, is the extent to which a post-war generation of Italians were, at the very same time, yearning just as passionately for an escape from the "good taste" of Italian design and the incessant formality of the traditional Italian lifestyle.

From the "spaghetti Westerns" produced on their own soil, and from Hollywood's portrayal of rugged individualism, young Italians developed their obsession with American casualwear. As Renzo Rosso puts it: "When I was young, America was like, Mamma mia!, something everyone dreamed about every day. America showed us another world. A world we wanted to be part of." And jeans were a symbol of that world. When Rosso and others of this generation put on denim casualwear, they were taking off the constrictions of traditional Italian life. It is in this context that we can begin to understand the phenomenal rise of small Italian casualwear/workwear companies such as those founded by Goldschmied, Elio Fiorucci, and Rosso. But while based on an American model, their clothing was given a craftsmanship and finesse that only Italy could provide.

The other thing desperately lacking in Italy was a sense of fun. Italians are renowned for taking everything extremely seriously—politics, sex, football, wine, art, and, perhaps most of all, style. Here was an important vacuum that needed to be filled, and Diesel in particular evolved to fill it. Diesel's humor—which was "post-modern" before most had heard of the term—is bizarre and irreverent. It is present in Diesel's clothing design in subtle ways (from vests styled to resemble aircraft life jackets to T-shirts embellished with shark warnings), but its expression is at its clearest in Diesel's communications.

Fun and casual, Diesel products are very Italian in their anti-Italianness. But since 1991, when it launched a worldwide advertising campaign and distribution system, Diesel's real success

"When I was young, America was something everyone dreamed about. America showed us another world."

Classic Diesel: jeans detail and retro pocket tags.

9

has been international. When Renzo Rosso took control in 1985, the company sold almost exclusively in Italy; today, the home market represents only 15 percent of sales. It is amusing to reflect that an Italian company, which was founded on an Italian dream of Americana, is now selling some 40 million dollars' worth of goods per year in the U.S. alone.

Diesel has now become a global company producing a global product—one that, increasingly, takes its inspiration from Europe, Asia, Australia, and the Third World, as well as from the U.S. As Rosso puts it: "Diesel is a giant tree. The roots are Italian, but as it has grown, each new branch has emerged representing a different nationality. We are English, Dutch, German, Japanese, Swedish, American—you name it." Rosso sees this multi-nationality as a crucial factor in Diesel's growth. "The obvious triumphs of this nationless, raceless company make a very attractive statement about the benefits of seeing the planet as without strict divisions—not 'us and them,' but simply one giant 'we.'"

All, presumably, wearing Diesel clothing in preparation for interplanetary integration.

Diesel as design

As soon as Renzo Rosso assumed complete control over Diesel, he went about transforming the company's approach to design—in ways that are still revolutionary by fashion industry standards.

"I hired some open-minded new stylists whose basic design preferences closely mirrored mine. I encouraged this group to ignore current movements within the fashion mainstream, and instead to focus their energies on producing a line which would accurately reflect who we were as people. I wanted clothing inspired by our own combined interests, tastes, and sense of curiosity." Rosso was happy with the existing Diesel product, but he was determined that their designs could be more original—more suited to an independent, stylistically creative customer. And so he gave broad stylistic freedom to everyone on the design team. "I promised everyone in the studio that I would manufacture only what proved to be the most innovative and fresh—not the safest or most easily sold—designs we came up with."

The approach was a great success. "Competing labels witnessed our dramatically improving fortunes and began to research, then copy, the Diesel model," recalls Rosso. "Fortunately for us, nearly everyone found our methods to be too unrealistic to duplicate. Our practice of preceding the market instead of following it, offering progressive styles before there was a proven demand for them, was something that could be pulled off only by a company willing to risk its future upon the instinct of its designers. Our rivals examined us looking for a magic formula, but discovered nothing more than a group of passionate people taking big chances, believing in themselves, and trusting their guts."

Discussing next season's designs at Diesel's Molvena headquarters.

"Diesel is a giant tree. The roots are Italian, but as it has grown, each new branch has emerged representing a different nationality."

Despite the freedom this approach offers, Diesel designers have inevitably faced a major obstacle: how to keep abreast of changing trends while geographically separated from Milan and the other fashion capitals of the world. The answer has been to turn a problem into an advantage. As Marly Nijssen, designer of Diesel Females, explains: "Because we're not in the center of where it's all happening in the fashion world, we're not so likely to just go with the flow. We're not influenced by the things that everybody else gets excited about. But we all travel a lot and that plugs us into the world. In the last four months, I've been to Morocco, Holland, Belgium, Hawaii, Bali, Singapore, Tokyo, L.A., Miami, and London."

Indeed, each designer at Diesel is provided with the funding for at least two "research expeditions" per year, to anywhere they want to go in the world. Chief designer Wilbert Das explains: "On these expeditions the designers buy clothes, books, magazines, music, postcards—whatever catches their eye, anything that will give them ideas. When they come back, they throw everything on the floor, mix it all up. Then everything gets hung on a rail, and the new season has started." The designers retreat to Renzo Rosso's nearby farm to think, to be in the sun, and to collect their ideas. "Down on the farm, things get very eclectic," says Das. "Somebody who has been to Alaska will be working with someone who has been to Honolulu. What's weird is that often the same type of things come back from completely different parts of the world. This synergy is a sign of the times—these global times."

An additional innovation at Diesel concerns the way the design studio is structured. "Here, the designer does everything from A to Z," points out Nijssen. "In most other companies, a designer produces sketches and from there other people will work on them, developing fabrics, production techniques, and so forth. The fact that here we do the whole process makes it easier to insist on something. You can look for solutions on the spot. You end up with fewer compromises and more integrity."

The result of all these innovations in design strategy is a product that, at least in comparison with most other mass-market clothing companies, is fresh, distinctive, complex, amusing, innovative, and flexible.

Diesel as brand

"We don't do advertising, we do communication—which we see as our 'face.' The product is the communication and the communication is also the product. It's all a system—a way to live, 'Successful Living'—which we and the customer create together. Our communication and our clothing are one and the same thing." The speaker is Maurizio Marchiori, Diesel's advertising and communications director. Undoubtedly, many within the

Eclectic influences: the 1989 "Valve" waistcoat, far left, derived its inspiration from anti-shark gear and pilots' uniforms; it also inflates like a mattress. The plastic quilting of babies' mats provided the spark for the women's jacket, left, from 1995.

fashion establishment would react to his words with horror. But to do so overlooks two important points. Firstly, the importance of marketing image is hardly a new phenomenon in fashion; Coco Chanel, for one, was at least as skilled at creating a "face" for her company as she was at designing. Secondly, the "keep fashion about fashion" approach ignores the extraordinary extent to which today's clothing exists and functions as communication.

In an ever more fragmented and heterogeneous world, we all need to be able to send out instant visual signals that explain "where we are at." Branding allows an enormous amount of information to be transmitted in our appearance, with the entire marketing image of a company being compacted into a recognizable style or logo. When we choose to wear certain brands, this information becomes part of our own "advertising" campaign, our own logo. For those who want to project a certain off-the-wall, surreal, knowing, and ironic image, the Diesel brand is priceless.

The special quality of Diesel's communication derives from the unique way that the company has structured its advertising team. Marchiori explains: "When in 1990 we realized that we needed to communicate, we were determined that this communication wouldn't become something separate from ourselves, our company, and our philosophy. Most clothing companies hire an outside advertising company and let them get on with it. What we did was to set up a creative team comprising those who know Diesel inside out—Renzo Rosso, myself, our head designer, and so on—together with ad agency people who were prepared to work with us on such a regular basis that they, in a sense, would become Diesel 'insiders.' We don't just brief an agency; we make tight, intimate contact. We never have ideas imposed from outside; the ideas always come from the heart of Diesel itself."

It was this creative team that came up with the "Successful Living" concept. "We wanted to find something different, something that had our humor, our sense of irony, our sense of fun," continues Marchiori. "The result was 'Successful Living'—a concept that has become a real part of the company. It worked because it's us, because it wasn't just tacked on from outside."

As Diesel continues to stack up advertising industry awards, some might ask whether the company's communication is beginning to outshine its product. Renzo Rosso is quick to respond: "People who say that our advertising is better than our product are missing the point. We win awards for our advertising, yes, but that is just because in the 1990s we have succeeded in making our advertising almost as good as our clothing." But to return to Maurizio Marchiori's slightly different perspective: in today's world it really has become unnecessary and undesirable—perhaps even impossible—to separate "product" from "communication." Where Diesel really stands out is precisely in its long-standing capacity to fuse together garments and lifestyle image.

Press advertisements from Diesel's groundbreaking "Successful Living" campaign. From left: "Don Juan" (1996), "Family Values" (1995), "How to Make Love Pay" (1993).

"We never have ideas imposed from outside; the ideas always come from the heart of Diesel itself."

All this might be unsettling were it not for the fact that Diesel seems consistently willing to mock itself. "A special thing about Diesel," argues Renzo Rosso, "is that we're prepared to laugh at ourselves. In this we are honest. The important thing is that it is our own sense of humor; the face we put on is our face." Rosso credits his parents: "They taught me to be honest, to be yourself. We're just taking this and putting it on a company level. And it works for the same reasons that it works in private life."

More successful living

Diesel began with two rooms, 20 sewing machines, and a telephone, selling jeans and trousers only in Italy. Today, as well as its enormous factory, warehouse, and headquarters, Diesel has over 20 flagship stores of its own, in cities including New York, London, San Francisco, Barcelona, Berlin, and Rome. There are also some 11,000 outlets for Diesel products in 82 countries. There is even a Diesel hotel in Miami. As well as continuing to produce a large jeans "Basics" line, Diesel now has extensive collections of designer/casual clothes for women and men (Diesel Style Lab); the Diesel Kids line; Spare Parts (accessories); a leather collection; and, since 1994, 55-DSL, an advanced sportswear line. The company has expanded successfully.

This last addition has come from Renzo Rosso's new-found enthusiasm for snowboarding—a sport well catered for in the mountains above Diesel's base town. "55-DSL is a more technical line than Diesel itself," explains designer Paul Thompson, himself an enthusiastic snowboarder. "A lot of sportswear up until now has been just logo-based. We're trying to play with new technologies and move away from a traditional 'sportswear' look." With technical input from experts and sports champions, this is a distinctive approach. "We're not losing Diesel's innovative philosophy, but at 55-DSL we take sports seriously." An unusual stance for Diesel, of course.

With all this expansion and diversification, one wonders what Diesel will do next. "We have to constantly keep moving," says Renzo Rosso. "We want to grow, but to be more exclusive at the same time. This isn't a contradiction. We want to have more of our own stores so as to show much more of who we are, to be more true to our own approach. This is what I mean by being exclusive—to be true to ourselves." So what of the Diesel future? "Every day we're looking for what is not done. We always look forward. What is done is done, but what is not done is our next great adventure. And I can tell you what won't happen. As long as I'm sitting at this desk, I can tell you that Diesel will never lose its sense of humor, its heart. The day I don't work any more from the heart, when I'm just working for the stocks and shares and all that, then I can't see any reason to keep doing it at all. It would seem too much like work. That's when I retire to my farm."

"Paveway" sneakers, a classic design from 1997.

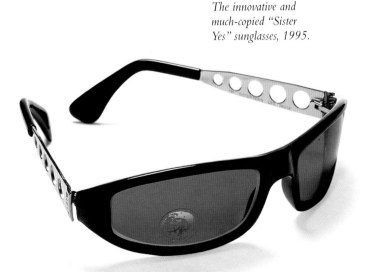

Diesel branches out. The innovative and much-copied "Sister Yes" sunglasses, 1995.

Designed for extreme sports: 55-DSL hat, 1998.

13

Nothing is what it seems

DIESEL'S MEN'S COLLECTION designer, Leo Brancovich, is getting excited as he shows me a new pair of trousers he's created. "You see these circular patterns? They're derived from some minefield mapping diagrams in an armored personnel carrier crew manual I found in Alaska. They're combined with material from a Russian 'G' suit. Of course, you don't have to know that. Maybe you just think they're a good pair of pants with a nice design. But for me, there's a special kick in knowing that they're actually something else entirely."

Leo has brought his sketch and the tank manual that inspired it into the bar of the Diesel's headquarters. Around us are fake windows that look beyond to picture-postcard views of Alpine mountains (when, in truth, outside are rolling Italian hills). Next, Marly Nijssen, designer of Diesel's women's collection, shows off a "bullet-proof vest" from last season. "Of course, it's not actually bullet-proof," she points out. "It was just the styling of bullet-proof vests that interested us." "Mind you," enthuses Leo, "it might be fun to make something that was actually bullet-proof, but which looked totally frivolous. Bullet-proof bikinis or ties. By the way, have you seen the new line of jumpers [sweaters] we've done which are perfectly clean, but look like they're covered in layers of scum and dirt?"

One is reminded of the novel *Against Nature* by J. K. Huysmans, in which the wonderfully perverse central character creates a conservatory with, on one side, fake flowers that look real and, on the other, real flowers that look like fakes. As in Huysmans' novel, nothing at Diesel is quite what it seems.

NOT SO HEAVY METAL
Fall/winter 1998

The permanently crumpled look is achieved by means of a thin metal mesh woven within the fabric.

OLD FOR NEW
Fall/winter 1998

Appearances deceive: this well-worn denim skirt is, in fact, brand new.

"NEW CLEAR POWER UNIT" BAG
Fall/winter 1998

"New Clear" as opposed to nuclear, this bag is actually radiation-free.

15

"ESSENTIAL WORDS AND PHRASES"
Clothing catalog, 1996

How to make friends abroad, the Diesel way. Cleverly disguised as a phrase book, this clothing catalog tells you how to ask "Where is the blacksmith?" in three languages.

"FIGHT ME"
Clothing catalog, 1997

Diesel presented its spring/summer 1997 collection in the form of "A Beginner's Guide to Self-Defense," which, among other things, demonstrated how to deal with a potential assailant who mails himself to your address disguised as a parcel.

In 1996, Diesel published a handbook, *Essential Words and Phrases for Travelers and Tourists,* which helpfully provides translations of phrases such as: "Please remove the fetid carcass from the bedroom," "Her skin has a purple hue," and "Excuse me, you are treading on my hand." This was followed by *Fight Me: Diplomacy Is a Kick in the Face,* described as "A Beginner's Guide to Self-Defense," by Wentworth K. Lee, whose maniacally smiling face appears on the cover. Both books turn out to be clothing catalogs, but close examination and an appreciation of Diesel's bizarre humor is necessary in order to grasp this fact. In 1998, in a new twist, Diesel ran a series of advertisements that all appeared to be pages from catalogs—but catalogs for television sets, cars, and gardening equipment.

PRESS ADS
Spring/summer 1998

Diesel clothing finds its way into a series of incongruous catalog spreads, including "Car Dealer" ("all models are available at your local showroom"), "Your Guide to Choosing the Latest Top Quality Gear," and "Lawn Care."

"PLUS PLUS"
Masculine and feminine fragrance, 1997

In yet another exercise in dissimulation, Diesel perfume comes in the guise of a milk bottle. At least you can open the carton without squirting its contents everywhere.

Q: When is a fashion catwalk show not a fashion catwalk show?

A: When Diesel turns the tables on the audience and makes them walk a catwalk themselves, with models inspecting them as they pass by. Positioned in a labyrinth of rooms—with names such as "Space Lab," "Bamboo Chopsticks," and "My Life as a Mermaid"—the models were actually "real life" wearers of Diesel, cast largely from London's streets and clubs.

One of the best-known Diesel commercials is set in India and features a certain Mr. Philips who clearly thinks he's Elvis Presley. "Mr. Philips" explains that he is the manufacturer of the "superdenim" from which Diesel jeans are made—a material that withstands our narrator's energetic rubbing of his backside on an abrasive wall and that, we are told, "dries in five or six seconds." "Not forgetting," he reminds us at the end, "it's good for your love life too." The ad is, of course, a pastiche, but what is particularly interesting is its inversion of values—many jeans companies that manufacture their products in the Far East would love to claim (as Diesel rightly could) that their jeans are made in Italy.

In other Diesel commercials, completely fictitious products are advertised, including Diesel hairspray, Diesel breath freshener, and Diesel "55" washing detergent. It should come as no surprise, therefore, that when Diesel launched its own perfume in 1997, it was packaged to look like a carton of milk. But then what can you expect of a company with a director who, in T-shirt, jeans, and cowboy boots, looks like he is there to clean the windows?

"HOT COUTURE"
Cinema/TV commercial, 1995

An entire Indian cinema epic packed into a 60-second commercial, "Hot Couture," maintains that Diesel's "No Problem Jeans for No Problem People" hail from Asia.

The global village

I T WAS, OF COURSE, Marshall McLuhan who foresaw the world becoming a "global village." In shaping Diesel, Renzo Rosso has put this theory into practice. That this should be accomplished from a small town in northern Italy—rather than, say, New York, London, or Tokyo—underlines the significance of this accomplishment (as well as the astuteness of McLuhan's original vision).

"Our biggest success," Rosso explains, "stems from the fact that we think internationally. Even in the beginning, we were global. Fifteen years ago it was kind of hard—especially in this small village. These people coming over here from England, from Holland, from Japan—they were like extraterrestrials."

But the people of Bassano del Grappa got used to these exotic creatures and soon found themselves home to a small but growing company that, both in its creative input and in its output, effectively spanned the globe. There is an irony at the heart of Diesel's global strategy,

however. Wilbert Das, one of the first Diesel "extraterrestrials" and now head of all design departments, explains: "Diesel is an Italian company in its appreciation of creativity—which means investing in good design, even if it does not immediately seem like good business—and in its constant experimentation with manufacturing techniques, always making them better and better." But the least Italian aspect of Diesel, says Das, is Renzo Rosso himself. "His attitude is completely global; he has never focused on Italy. He believes in making the same product for everybody. People in Malaysia see the same things on TV as people in California; Renzo realized that they can wear the same clothing, too." As Rosso puts it: "We at Diesel view the world as a single, borderless macro-culture."

At the same time, however, Diesel has always been quick to derive inspiration from specific cultures. In clothing design, ideas may come from Japan, the U.S., Cuba, Bali, Alaska, and Hawaii—all within a single season. But

WORLD VIEW
1990 and 1994
catalogs

The idea of planet Earth as seen from outer space has been a recurring visual theme for Diesel catalogs. "Vacation 1994" gives a tourist's-eye view of fashion.

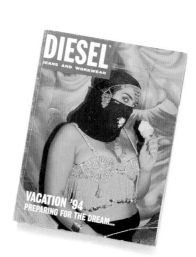

DIESEL GOES
HAWAIIAN
1991 catalog

Diesel designers have long held a special affection for the bright, classic prints of Hawaiian shirts, seen here in the spring/ summer 1991 catalog. Today, however, the aim is increasingly to search out more unexpected, less stereotyped inspirations from Hawaii and elsewhere.

AWAPUHI LAU PALA WALE

"the ginger leaf... wilts quickly"

ASIAN MIX
Fabric details, spring/summer
1998

The textile designs for many of the shirts, T-shirts, and jackets in this collection were inspired by designers' trips to Japan, Indonesia, and China.

WEST MEETS EAST
1998 catalog

Motifs with a Far East feel were printed on nylon sports fabric for the men's and women's spring/summer 1998 collection.

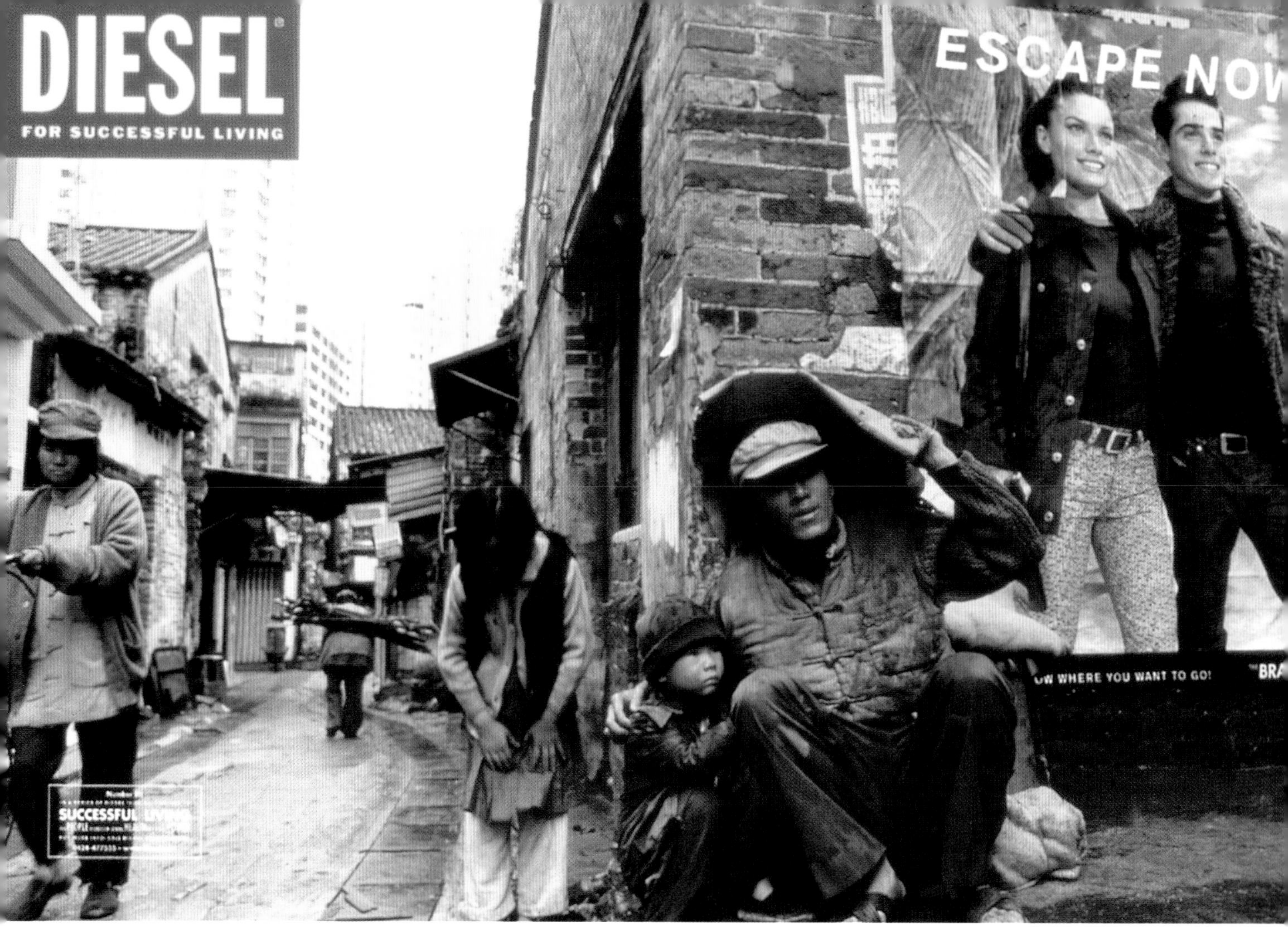
DIESEL
FOR SUCCESSFUL LIVING
ESCAPE NOW
OW WHERE YOU WANT TO GO!
SUCCESSFUL

"ESCAPE NOW"
Press advertisement, 1997

A different view of Asia. Diesel set its fall/winter 1997 campaign in North Korea, but did not run the advertisements in China or Japan.

Diesel never employs such references in a straightforward way. A summer shirt, for instance, reflects both the beauty and the tackiness of foreign travel by combining its South Seas influence with a photo-print from packaging found in Singapore. Ethnic references always have a twist: the "batik" is just pretend; a bamboo print is somewhat unexpectedly found on natural wool.

Diesel's advertisements, likewise, may take us to Africa or India, Switzerland or France, but we always remain firmly within "The World According to Diesel." The ironic, surreal twist, the use of colors that are a shade too bright, or black and white that is a little too *noir*, converts America into "America," Japan into "Japan," France into "France." It is a world within quotation marks—also the defining characteristic, according to cultural theorists, of the post-modern condition.

In "The World According to Diesel," culturally specific stylistic identities have become like costumes for a fancy dress party, which can be changed, combined, or discarded on a whim. Diesel design proceeds from the premise that people today have a more flexible and more playful relationship with their country of origin. "The boundaries between nations are losing their tendency to act as borders of the mind, borders which in years past may have locked people into limited, predictable ways of thinking—or dressing," says Rosso. "As these divisions become less important, cultures begin overlapping one another. Today, a group of teenagers chosen at random from different parts of the world are likely to share many of the same specific tastes and interests. They may have the same favorite television program or musical group, follow the success of the same athletes and sports teams; they may lust after the same supermodel, worship the same film stars, or even be crazy about wearing the same brand of jeans. And guess what brand I would like that to be."

"MAGIC 55"
Cinema/TV commercial, 1994

Diesel traveled to Japan to advertise a completely fictional product, but never, of course, left planet Diesel. A giant TV billboard behind the girls shows an earlier Diesel ad, "Clean Family Fun," while 1955 is the year Renzo Rosso was born.

Time travel

A FEW MILES away from the Diesel head-quarters there is a huge "museum" housing row after row of garments brought back by designers on research expeditions. There are representative samples here, not only from all four corners of the globe, but also from every post-war decade. On one rack is a collection of those Italian sweaters from the 1950s that so excited the British Mods, alongside American motorcycle jackets and a huge collection of original Hawaiian shirts. From the 1960s is a pair of denim bellbottoms so patched that little denim is visible, Mod garments from "Swinging London," Afghan coats, and Swedish army surplus. Things get funky in the 1970s section; then punk, the new romantics, goths, and skinheads all make an appearance before things settle down into various 1980s styles: everything from yuppie to hip-hop. On an upper floor, original Diesel garments—some famous classics, many undeveloped prototypes—trace out their own history.

Just as Diesel does not restrict its inspiration within geographic borders, so too does it freely indulge its taste for time travel. Perhaps this was inevitable for a company that began by producing denim jeans, a garment steeped in historic, American "Wild West" associations. Looking through Diesel's old catalogs, as in browsing through its "museum," one can see that Diesel's designers have traveled as extensively through time as they have through space.

Indeed, there are those who criticize Diesel for simply copying vintage garments. A close look at Diesel's own output, however, reveals that few, if any, garments are "retro" in a direct sense. Much more evident is that "temporal dislocation," which, if post-modern theorists are to be believed, has become a typical feature of our world today. Stylistic features from the 1950s, for instance, might be juxtaposed with fabrics,

NOW AND THEN
Diesel makes history

Decade-hopping, Diesel style. While the in-store material (left) **and the 1989 catalog spread** (right) **both draw inspiration from the 1950s, the print used on the classic Diesel shirt** (below) **is derived from an early 1960s curtain design. Note how Diesel manages two completely different recreations of the 1950s: one "street," the other "high fashion."**

ONLY THE
BRAVEST
1989 catalog

Transporting us back to the days of the "Wild West," Diesel gets cowboys and Native Americans to mingle peacefully.

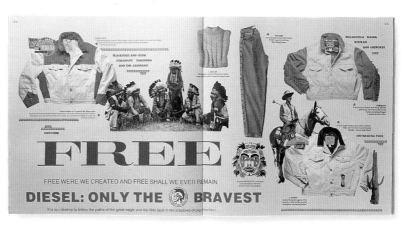

FREE WERE WE CREATED AND FREE SHALL WE EVER REMAIN

DIESEL: ONLY THE BRAVEST

It is our destiny to follow the paths of the great eagle and the little bear in the shadows of pig mountain

GLITTER ON
Fall/winter 1998

1970s glitter overlaid on minimal military forms gives a 1990s feel to this T-shirt.

NEW AGE ANORAK
Fall/winter 1998

1950s anorak meets 1980s "puffer" jacket for this contemporary design.

VINTAGE JEANS
Bought in the U.S.

Picked up on one of Diesel's "research expeditions," a pair of jeans that might well have seen Woodstock now hang in the Molvena archive alongside leather biker jackets and workmen's overalls.

YALTA, 1945
Press advertisement, Historic Moments series, 1997

Like the thought-police in George Orwell's *1984*, Diesel has the ability to rewrite history. No doubt its sexier version of the Yalta Conference could have averted the Cold War.

DIESEL HISTORICAL MOMENTS:

BIRTH OF THE MODERN CONFERENCE, YALTA, 1945.

DIESEL HISTORICAL MOMENTS:
JOB INTERVIEW, ARMY RECRUITMENT SERVICES, 1960.

As with geography, the "Dieselization" of history gives the past an ironic and surreal twist. "Job Interview, Army Recruitment Services, 1960" *(left)* helpfully tells us that "the position will ideally suit an ambitious individual now wishing to increase their strategic capacity," while "UN Development Office, Monrovia, 1955" *(below)* gives an unusual slant on twentieth-century world politics.

*Retro Diesel
ashtray, 1991*

DIESEL HISTORICAL MOMENTS:
U.N. DEVELOPMENT OFFICE, MONROVIA, 1955.

That's not a bad idea, Miss Nelson. We'll pass it on to the board in Cairo. You never know, they might even work it into the agenda at conference level, and we may eventually receive some funding to form a research committee down here. Now, let's focus on the cocktail party we're throwing to welcome you to Africa. It would probably be a good idea if you dressed in red, don't you think?

colors, or patterns from the 1970s. For the fall/winter 1998 collection, futuristic fabrics take on 1980s details—such as ruching, diamante, and boat-necks—while the trousers are a 1970s shape. Diesel design "surfs" history as promiscuously and as casually as it "surfs" geography, delighting in unexpected juxtapositions.

It is the same story when it comes to Diesel's communications. The 1970s funksters of the commercial "Le Look Le Plus Cool"; the 1950s styling of "Clean Family Fun" (see page 38); and the entire "Diesel Historic Moments" series of classic still images (from the Yalta conference to a beauty contest line-up) with Diesel-clad models imposed upon them, are just a few examples from many. Like Diesel designs themselves, all perfectly illustrate that generic "ahistory" which is such a central feature of our post-modern age.

However, while Diesel has been doing the time-warp with the best of them, indications are that this may be changing. "For me, the retro thing is slowing down a bit," says head designer Wilbert Das. "The 'casual boom' in the 1980s was grounded in an all-pervasive retro obsession, especially in Italy and France. It was very stimulating for a while, forcing us to look carefully at what vintage styles had to offer. But now we're just as likely to look to the future—through technological advances in fabrics, for example—or sideways into other areas." Das puts some of this down to the fast-approaching millennium, but doesn't regret the past. "I think it's right that we once relied heavily on retro styles—we've got a whole museum to prove it! But what point is there in a 1990s revival before we're even out of that same decade?"

"BATTLE OF THE ARDENNES"
Cinema/TV commercial, 1997

Gritty black-and-white realism gives a documentary feel to this bizarre commercial which, in the end, turns out to be a disturbing and surreal fantasy.

Sampling & mixing

TODAY WE LIVE in a "surfing" culture, zapping between different TV channels, Internet sites, ideas, people. And styles.

Appearance—how we choose to look—has always had an almost uncanny way of mirroring the spirit of the times. In the modern world (from the early Renaissance up until recently), fashion decreed a single "direction" and more or less everyone followed its lead. Now, in postmodern times, this consensus has been broken, things have become more fragmented, heterogeneous, chaotic—and also more interesting.

In popular music today, we see a new method of creation: music is sampled from eclectic sources and mixed together to make something new. It is the same with visual style. Most people we see on the street, in the supermarket, in a nightclub, rather than conforming to a single fashion "direction," will bring together in their appearance all sorts of different elements— the more diverse, the better.

But many in the fashion industry seem not to have caught on. They persist in thinking that if "brown is the new black," then people will throw away every item of clothing that is the "wrong" color. Equally, there are still those who believe that the designer has the right—indeed, the responsibility—to dictate a "total look." But today, it is only the most unimaginative "fashion victims" who will allow themselves to be controlled in this manner. Nowadays, the consumer is an intrinsic part of the creative fashion process.

One of the things that is special about Diesel is that it readily and openly recognizes that fashion (or style, a more appropriate term) now operates according to new rules—rules that respect the aesthetic sensibilities of the consumer as well as the designer.

I shop therefore I am: mannequins pose as customers in the Berlin store.

DUFFEL BAG AND T-SHIRT
Fall/winter 1996 (bag); fall/winter 1989 (T-shirt)

Diesel's offbeat sources of inspiration positions the company well away from the fashion mainstream. A medical blanket is transformed into a duffel bag (above), **while shark warnings and military stenciling emblazon a T-shirt** (below).

ON THE CATWALK
Fall/winter 1997

Typical of Diesel's eclectic output, this collection offers consumers a host of opportunities for mixing up a distinctive look.

ALL MIXED UP
Men's jacket, 1993

In the early days, Diesel designers would "customize" archive pieces by mixing elements from different garments. This hybrid combines a nylon sports jacket and a woollen ski sweater, embellished on the sleeves with ice hockey protection patches.

DIESEL POWERED
Men's jacket, 1991

A traditional leather motorcycle jacket is appliquéd with publicity graphics from a car parts manufacturer. A pair of leather trousers provided inspiration for the elbow patches.

WAR GAMES
Spring/summer 1998

Western military styling given an Eastern twist: a Japanese tiger motif is combined with combat detailing and a metallic sports fabric.

SPORTY CATS
Spring/summer 1998

The Asian tiger here lends a Far Eastern feel to a traditional basketball shirt.

   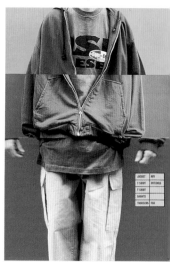

5 5 - D S L
1994 catalog

These images—showing the first 55-DSL collection—graphically illustrate the way in which the Diesel consumer is perceived as a creative part of the "sampling and mixing" process.

"Every collection has 1,200 combinations of color, style, and fabric per season," explains Renzo Rosso. "It's one of the unique things about Diesel. It's important because it allows the consumer some flexibility, some creativity in putting a look together." Diesel is in tune with today's style-conscious consumer. "We want to give the consumer a chance to express him- or herself. People today will not accept being dictated to, controlled. At Diesel we have very imaginative designers—and very imaginative consumers. We don't want to transform the customer into simply being an instrument of our own vision."

Marly Nijssen of Diesel Females expresses a similar view: "I think it's very boring when people wear just one brand from top to bottom. I love it when I see people taking our stuff and putting it together with other things. That's the kind of person we like designing for. We design garments, not whole outfits—that's for people

with little imagination. And Diesel customers certainly have a lot of imagination."

Sampling and mixing is also a very good way to describe the creative process at Diesel. As head designer Wilbert Das puts it: "We collect stuff, we mix it up—always giving it a twist, at the very least putting a different conceptual frame around it to give it a different meaning. More often we completely deconstruct something. We go crazy. We take things from different cultures, from different eras, and throw them all together to make something new, something pleasantly confusing."

Ours is an amazingly eclectic world, with diverse ideas, perspectives, and styles constantly colliding as if in some giant atom smasher. Instead of being frustrated by this state of affairs, Diesel long ago recognized this fact of (postmodern) life and embraced it enthusiastically. As in contemporary pop music, everything at Diesel is "in the mix."

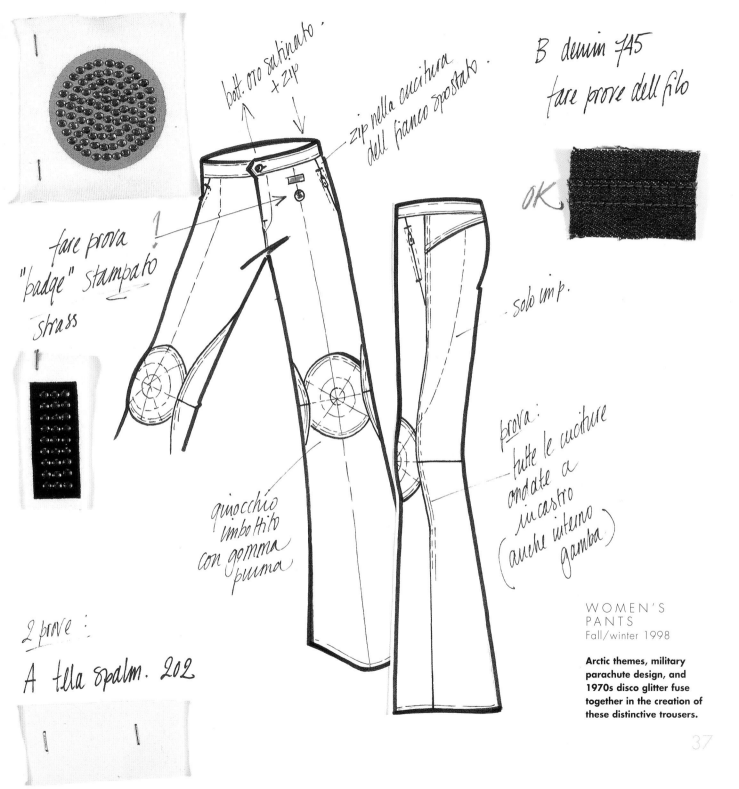

bott. oro satinato · + zip

zip nella cucitura dell fianco spostato ·

B denim 745 fare prove dell filo

OK.

fare prova "badge" stampato strass

solo imp.

ginocchio imbottito con gomma puma

prova: tutte le cuciture ondate a incastro (anche interno gamba)

2 prove:

A tela spalm. 202

WOMEN'S PANTS
Fall/winter 1998

Arctic themes, military parachute design, and 1970s disco glitter fuse together in the creation of these distinctive trousers.

37

ITALY HAS LONG BEEN a place where men, as well as women, care passionately about their appearance. Diesel may well have been founded in a spirit of reaction to sartorial formality, but its casual approach was never in opposition to the peacock-like tendencies of the Italian male. Far from it: a cross between Mastroianni in *La Dolce Vita* and Brando in *The Wild One*, Diesel Man combines the sensual qualities of the Latin lover with the rough-and-ready tradition founded in the Wild West, which lives on (trading the horse for a motorcycle) in the form of the Biker Outlaw.

Consider one of the earliest Diesel cinema/TV advertisements, "Clean Family Fun." Here, we jump between a prim but pretty 1950s housewife, who is seen fanatically dusting and vacuuming the family home, and a rakishly handsome, Diesel-clad young man on a motorcycle who goes off to fill a large bag with freshly dug dirt. Roaring up on his bike, our hero defiantly strides across a pristine white carpet, leaving muddy footprints in his wake. He then proceeds to dump a large bag of dirt in the center of the carpet, kicking it about a bit for good measure. At first, we think this dastardly character has deliberately spoiled all this nice woman's work. But no—she and the entire extended family are delighted. Now, like Sisyphus, they can begin their task afresh. This, then, is yet another example of successful living, the Diesel way: the male exuberant in his dirty, naughty, but ultimately nice, ways.

Indeed, in most Diesel advertisements it is the male—casual, rough, yet smart as well as sexy—who saves the day. In "Love All Serve All," the male saves the damsel from being ravished by a terrible monster. In "The End," it is the male who initially seems to be the monster (apparently, a chainsaw-wielding psychopath), but all ends happily as he finally employs his chainsaw to cut an enormous birthday cake.

"CLEAN FAMILY FUN"
Cinema/TV commercial, 1992

He's a filthy, motorcycle-riding devil. She's a pretty, prim and pristine 1950s housewife. In "The World According to Diesel," such opposites attract and live happily ever after—successfully.

CHILL OUT
Catalog image, fall/winter 1998

Diesel Man and Diesel Woman have been through a lot together. While previously their coupling has often been too hot to handle, here they enter a new ice age—in style and unison. (Photograph by Rankin.)

FEMININE

Today's Working Woman wants to look wonderful both on and off the job. Diesel will reassure her with stunning styles and fabulous fabrics. It's easy, because Diesel always knows how.

OUR QUALITY IS REAL

GOOD

THE WORKING WOMAN

NOT IN THE SOUTH

40

None of which is very surprising for a company that began making products only for men. What is interesting, however, is that throughout its communications history, Diesel has also portrayed women as strong, independent, and fiendishly smart. In the very first Diesel cinema/TV advertisement, an attractive young woman—dressed in tight Diesel jeans, of course—stands by the side of a road smiling provocatively at passing male drivers. What she (and we) know is that just ahead there is a dangerous curve in the road. Crash. Bang. Our heroine pries the inner tubes from the crashed cars for her and her happy family to use in their swimming pool. Another case of successful living the Diesel way—this time, with female cunning saving the day.

What began as a purely male product was matched, in the late 1980s, by a women's range.

As designer Marly Nijssen explains: "When Diesel started, there was no casual clothing specifically made for women. If you wanted to have this casual look, you had to buy men's clothing. What I wanted to do was to retain the classic male casual style, but to give it a new fit, designed specifically for women." At the same time, Diesel also sought to update the image of women in its communication. "We wanted to find a woman's look which would fit in with the 'Diesel Guy'—a woman who is as independent and clever as she is sexy. The criticism I've often heard of Diesel is that it's all about sex—which in a certain way is true. Our clothes have a lot of sex appeal. But it's not just about women's sexuality. At Diesel, it's both men and women who get to be sex objects."

If sexuality is not the sole preserve of either gender, neither are pragmatism and power.

DIESEL
FEMALES
1991 catalog

The soft-edged "working woman" contrasts markedly with the sexually up-front females seen in the "Successful Living" series, and the raunchy party animals of the spring/summer 1998 catalog (see page 43).

ROMANCE
EXPRESS
Press advertisements, 1992

"Diesel Man" meets "Diesel Woman" in "How to Date More Successfully" and "How to Understand Life on Earth." The toy boy on the blonde's thigh leaves no doubt as to who is in charge.

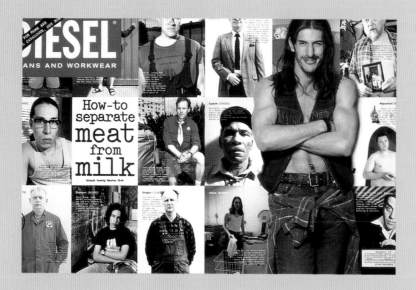

"DIESEL
LONELY
HEARTS
CLUB"
Press advertisement,
1993

"Mr. Right" likes
"foreign films and
clogs." The "hairy,
strong and politically
correct peanut
farmer" has a
problem with cats.
Mr. Diesel, however,
seems to have no
problems.

"HEY FOLKS!"
Press advertisement,
1992

Number 1 in Diesel's
"Successful Living"
series featured this
rather stereotyped
blonde. Subsequent
"Diesel Females,"
however, would include
kung fu-fighting Asians
and a funky girl with
a shaved head.

It is Marina Tosin, Diesel's female vice-president, who keeps Renzo Rosso in check: "I very much admire Renzo's talents, and particularly his good judgment with people, but that doesn't mean I restrain myself from disagreeing with him," says Tosin. "I'm a lot more pessimistic than he is, and we butt heads over the wisdom of some of his more daring business moves. It's two stubborn Italian personalities colliding, and things often get a bit heated. I listen, he listens, and sometimes we come up with a mutual consensus, but often we just agree to disagree."

At Diesel, it seems, it is both Renzo Rosso and Marina Tosin who wear the trousers—Diesel jeans for both, of course.

PARTY ANIMALS
1998 catalog

In the late 1990s, Diesel has managed to turn the erotic temperature even higher. As usual, there are plenty of male, as well as female, objects of desire.

43

"HOW TO TEACH your children to love and care. Modern children need to SOLVE their <u>OWN</u> problems: teaching kids to KILL helps them deal <u>directly</u> with reality—but they learn SO much quicker when you give them a guiding hand! Make them proud and confident! Man, if they never learn to blast the brains out of their neighbors what kind of damn <u>FUTURE</u> has this COUNTRY of ours got???"

Number 15 in Diesel's "Successful Living" advertisement series drew an enormous response. Letters of protest poured into the Diesel offices and irate pickets protested outside Bloomingdales, the exclusive outlet for Diesel products at that time. The advertisement's ironic humor had obviously not been wholeheartedly appreciated. "This was our first advertisement in the U.S. and we realized immediately that we had been too strong, too quickly," says Maurizio Marchiori. "We realized that we had to work harder to prepare the way for this sort of stuff."

Diesel's communication is nothing if not provocative. "Our ironic tone sometimes initially shocks consumers," admits Renzo Rosso. "We often present what appear to be outrageously inappropriate messages—confusing references to such things as racial and sexual stereotypes, materialism, drug abuse, religious intolerance, and political extremism. A person must think a bit in order to decide what the treatment of these subjects is intended to prompt them to feel. But once they have taken the time to make a considered response, the viewer of a Diesel ad usually—though admittedly not always—picks up on a hidden order behind the work, a meaning that is less an insensitive, subjective statement, and more a balanced observation of the realities of the world we share."

Diesel's communication always strives to work on at least two levels, often seemingly contradictory—one amusing and sexy, the other

"MAKE MY DAY"
Press advertisement, 1993

In suggesting that parents should teach their kids to use guns, number 15 in the "Successful Living" advertising series was obviously trying to make a point about gun control. Many readers, however, missed the irony.

ideological and thought-provoking. "Our publicity has attempted to direct attention toward a number of societal issues and accepted norms which we at Diesel feel could use some re-examination," declares Rosso.

Having shown a healthy disdain for political correctness, Diesel has also gone on to spit in the eye of "good taste." In magazines, which typically feature only beautiful people doing beautiful things, their images of pigs feasting on a pig laid out on an ornate dining table, excessively pumped-up body builders, wrinkled geriatric sun-worshippers, gold-painted old men in skimpy bathing suits, magnified slices of raw meat, and leering, obviously psychopathic dentists in sunglasses all stand out, to say the least.

But as shocking as Diesel advertisements can be, more often than not they manage to rise above a purely attention-getting level—either by containing a serious point of social concern or, simply but effectively, by causing us to ponder the meaning of life. No other clothing company would appear to offer such philosophical discourse. Heaven help us, however, if Diesel ever loses its sense of humor, starts taking itself too seriously, and organizes a religious cult.

"BUSINESS AS USUAL"
Cinema/TV commercial, 1998

Diesel's dislike of hypocrisy has never been clearer than in this 1998 commercial, in which a pornographer turns out to be a pillar of the community with a "Family, Love, Morality" bumper sticker.

SLAUGHTERING SACRED COWS
Press advertisements, 1993–98

Apparently determined to offend, irritate, or shock just about everyone, Diesel's communications have never been known to pull their punches. Interestingly, the only one of these ads that caused Diesel any problems was "Smoke 145 a Day," which some magazines refused to carry for fear of losing cigarette advertisements.

Planet youth

DIESEL IS TYPICALLY seen as a "youth culture" design company. Certainly it is true that many of its core concepts relate particularly to the young. Statistically, too, the typical Diesel customer is under 25. But no one seems to have consciously planned things this way—the "youth market" is not specifically targeted. Indeed, just as Diesel realizes that national boundaries are increasingly becoming less significant, so too has the company recognized that how old you are is nowadays less important than how you think, what you do in your spare time, and how you dress.

"A lot of our customers are young, but we design for ourselves—and I'm now 42," says Renzo Rosso. "The important thing is to be young in mind. I have five children—one is 20 and one is 19 and we can go snowboarding or even to a club together. This is very different from when I was a boy. The 'generation gap' is over. The Diesel consumer is not limited by age."

Design head Wilbert Das backs this up: "When outside marketing people began coming to our company, they were asking, 'What is the age of your target market?' And we were like, 'Huh?' This isn't a 'youth' company in terms of age, in terms of numbers. It all has to do with a way of thinking—being young in your mind. There is no age at which you have to hang up your Diesel clothes. If there were, a lot of us who work at Diesel would be in trouble!"

In 1995, when Renzo Rosso turned 40, he published a huge, lavishly produced book—called *FoRty*—about himself, his friends and, of course, Diesel. Someone else running a company that attracts predominantly young customers might have tried to sweep middle age under the carpet. Not so Rosso, who celebrated with fireworks and a brass band. He explains how he manages to retain his youthful attitude: "When people in my business talk about the 'young generation,' 'today's youth,' 'kids of the 90s' and

To mark his fortieth birthday, Renzo Rosso published a lavish book, *FoRty* (below and opposite), which chronicled his own and Diesel's history. Far left: Renzo Rosso in 1967 and 1995; just how did they match the wallpaper?

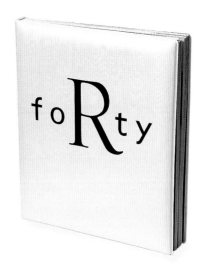

Keep ing up with the kids

When people in my business talk about the "young generation, today's youth, kids of the 90's etc.." I have a real advantage in knowing of whom they speak. It's not just because my company targets and sells products to these people, but because I've got two teenage sons: Stefano and Andrea. My boys and their friends are my No.1 source of information about youth culture and new trends. I can think of many specific areas where the kids' influence shows itself on me, some of the most obvious being my exposure to fresh developments in music and entertainment. As the young generation's taste in these things evolves, I'm always one of the first in my company to recognize the fresh movements. I usually hear rising, newly hip musicians on my boys' stereos at home or played in my car long before they arrive on the radio or music video channels. If there are movies, television shows, hobbies and games which are becoming popular for the young, I'm quickly aware of them as well; these subjects are frequently at the heart of conversations between Andrea, Stefano, and their buddies at our house in the evenings – often around the dinner table – or when we're all doing things together on weekends. Snowboarding, one of this generation's major emerging sports, is something I don't imagine I would ever have tried if the kids hadn't pushed me so hard into it. I now love the sport, though I admit I nearly killed myself learning it. I'm certainly not suggesting by all this that people in my industry should adopt teenagers as a 'research tool' (though they'd likely pick up some valuable insight if they did). My relationship with my children, of course, has a lot more substance than just the pursuit of free time activities we can enjoy together. As many things as I seem to discover from them, I hope they're learning a number of much more important lessons from me – such as how to get through this life in one piece and keep their heads on straight. All parents have an obligation to offer such guidance to their kids, but I often get the sense that I have significant advantages over some in approaching these issues with young people. After all, what could be more informative or convenient than the profession I'm in; work that encourages me to keep in close contact with – to research to the point of actually engaging myself in – all the endless variety of things my kids' generation finds interesting? I believe I'll always relate better with my three children because of it.

DIESEL KIDS
Fall/winter 1997
catalog

In both its clothing design and its communication, Diesel refuses to treat kids as if they were a separate species. This catalog was inspired by Lewis Carroll's *Alice in Wonderland* and is intended to conjure up the same feelings as that book: a mixture of fears, dreams, and wonderment.

DIESEL KIDS
Spring/summer 1997
catalog

As with the adult collections, Diesel Kids follows its own course of research, development, and image. "We never forget that Diesel boys and girls are not dolls," says designer Peter Kempkens. "Kids know what they want to wear, and how to wear it. We respect that."

so on, I have a real advantage in knowing whom they are speaking about. It's not just because my company sells products to these people, but because of my two sons. My boys and their friends are my number-one source of information about youth culture and new trends. Snowboarding, one of this generation's major emerging sports, is something I don't imagine I would ever have tried if the kids hadn't pushed me so hard into it. I now love the sport, though I admit I nearly killed myself learning it."

Youthful, but never ageist, Diesel—like Renzo Rosso—appears to have moved beyond the limitations of a "generation gap" mindset. Why then, one might wonder, are the exemplifiers of "successful living" in Diesel communications nearly always young, while those engaged in what is presumably unsuccessful living are often old? Communications head Maurizio Marchiori presents a spirited defense: "It isn't age itself that makes these characters absurd. They are right-wing generals looking ridiculous in a playpen, people who have done too much sunbathing, so their skin has gone prematurely wrinkled, fat men gorging themselves on huge plates of hamburgers and chips. It's militarism, excessive sunbathing, and gluttony that we're objecting to here, certainly not the age of the people involved."

At which point we have to end our interview so that Maurizio (aged 46) can join Renzo Rosso (aged 42) and others to play for Diesel's football team. Come winter, the whole Diesel staff will go snowboarding together.

"MERRY CHRISTMAS"
Press advertisement, 1995

All ages (and races) can settle down comfortably within The World According To Diesel.

"BABY GENERALS"
Press advertisement, 1994

Three generals in a playpen, wearing diapers, are watched over by a nanny and four sharply attired Diesel Females. Just where do they get the older models from, and what must they think of it all?

"SOLARIUM"
Press advertisement, 1994

Is this a clever public health warning, a joke at the expense of senior citizens, or just another surreal image from Diesel communications?

53

"ONE HUNDRED PERCENT Diesel" is what Renzo Rosso and his team say they are aiming for. Their "stores project"—establishing their own, purpose-built retail outlets around the world—is beginning to make this dream a reality. While their flagship shops in New York, London, Berlin, Paris, Barcelona, Rome, and San Francisco may all have distinctive looks, their atmosphere is nonetheless most certainly "one hundred percent Diesel."

"You need to be perfect in every aspect," says Rosso of his retail environments. "In the window, in every square foot of the store. Even ten years ago it was enough just to create the product and the advertising. Now you need to produce a total environment, a world in which everything fits together perfectly."

According to guidelines set out by Diesel's interior design department, the stores aim to be "privileged places where fashion, architecture, and design blend together in an experimental area of great interest." The stores are a "total environment"—that is, a totally Diesel environment where design trends get translated into three-dimensional spaces. To assist in accomplishing this, ideas are tested with state-of-the-art computer modeling software that simulates the movements of customers within the designed space.

"We started out just selling jeans, and now we're selling a way of life," says Rosso. The Diesel lifestyle can now be brought to your own home via the firm's Web site (at http://www.diesel.com), which even incorporates a home shopping service. "It's Diesel on your doorstep," declares new media manager Bob Shevlin. "Some people think that Internet shopping is the future of retailing, but for us right now, it's just a really entertaining and interesting way of letting people buy our product."

As well as running what may be the most comprehensive Web operation of any fashion company, Diesel is energetically participating in the latest generation of video games. The company has lent its stylistic expertise—and ironic sensibility—to the heroes of *G-Police* by Psygnosis, and is also producing a games-and-music-filled CD-ROM, *Digital Adrenaline 55-DSL*.

NEW YORK
STORE
Opened 1996

Diesel's flagship New York store marked a key point in the company's conquest of the U.S. Like all Diesel stores, it is designed to blend fashion, architecture, and design into a "total environment."

NEW YORK
STORE
INTERIOR
Computer-generated
rendering

**State-of-the-art technology
is used to create
individually tailored
interiors for each store.**

BELGRADE
STORE
INTERIOR
Computer-generated
rendering

**The virtual becomes more
of a reality—but to achieve
one hundred percent
Diesel, it will need
products and people.**

DIESEL
ONLINE
www.diesel.com, 1998

Diesel has an extensive presence on the Internet. A visitor can view Diesel fashion shows or make use of Diesel's "virtual store" to order clothing and accessories. The Web site also offers an index of shops, an opportunity for visitors to register their views on any subject, and an online guide to "successful shopping." But this isn't the end of Diesel's virtual story; by designing the clothes for characters in video games such as *G-Police*, Diesel cleverly achieves widespread product placement.

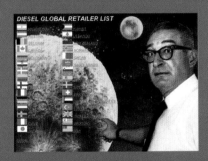

VARIETY, THE
SPICE OF LIFE
Interior, Diesel flagship store in New York

Every Diesel collection offers thousands of options of color, fabric, and style.

57

"We always try to promote Diesel in ways that will surprise customers, and which don't seem intrusive. Dressing the characters in video games, or putting Diesel billboards on streetscapes of games, only adds to the sense of realism, and improves the playing experience," says Shevlin. "Of course we approach this with the usual Diesel levity. If, for example, players have any reason not to like Diesel, they can usually blow up our shops or destroy our clothing."

For those wanting to "get real," there is always the Pelican Hotel in Miami, which Diesel acquired in 1991 and then redesigned. As one would expect from Diesel's eclectic, time-warping approach, each of the Pelican's rooms offers a completely different lifestyle experience—guests can choose between "Cubarean Islands," "Up, Up in the Sky," "Best Whorehouse," and "Power Flower," among others. The Pelican is both "one hundred percent Diesel" and sensitive to its unique location and history—its American and Caribbean furnishings are all original items that have been culled from a 60-year period and lovingly restored.

Such horizontal development has long been Diesel's developmental direction. While hardly unique to the company, it is Diesel's long-standing, explicit, and enthusiastic recognition of this trend that makes it an important visionary. This is the essence of what branding is all about—breaking down the boundaries, not only between clothing and furniture, for example, but also between designed objects and the philosophies that (through a total communications strategy) are embedded in them. Diesel is an important pioneer in its understanding of itself as more than a creator of garments.

The French philosopher Jean Baudrillard has prophesied that one day the entire world will become one giant theme park. If Renzo Rosso has his way (and he usually does), it will be called Dieseland and it will be a place of ironic humor, heartfelt intuition, and global thinking, where stylishly dressed people—young and old—will experience the delights of successful living. No doubt already, in some distant part of the galaxy on planet Diesel, they are toasting yet another successful interplanetary conquest.

For Successful Living

The heart-rending finale of this 1995 commercial pulls out all the stops— it even has a "Diesel Loves You" soundtrack.

PELICAN HOTEL
South Beach, Miami,
opened 1994

As with Diesel's fashion range, its hotel in Miami offers the customer maximum choice, with each room distinctively themed. All furnishings are restored originals found in the U.S. and the Caribbean.

59

Chronology

1863
Rudolph Diesel devises and patents an internal combustion engine (but fails to see the potential for launching a fashion design company).

1955
Renzo Rosso born in Brugine, near Padua, northern Italy.

1970
Renzo Rosso begins studies at Marconi (now Natta) Technical Institute, Padua.

1971
Renzo Rosso makes his first garment—a pair of bell-bottomed, low-waisted trousers. These are a great success with his friends.

1976
Renzo Rosso takes his first job in the clothing industry, working for Italian casual clothing pioneer Adriano Goldschmied in his company Moltex.

1978
Adriano Goldschmied and Renzo Rosso found Diesel as a new casual clothing brand among the Genius Group, an affiliation of 14 separate clothing labels, each with a unique style and concept.

1979
First complete Diesel men's collection produced.

1981
Diesel begins to export clothing outside Italy.

1984
First Diesel Kids line is produced.

1985
Renzo Rosso separates from the Genius Group and takes complete control of Diesel.

1987
Renzo Rosso buys his first Harley-Davidson motorcycle.

1989
Diesel Females is born.

1990
Diesel begins preparations for its first international advertising campaign.

1991
Diesel launches its "Successful Living" advertising campaign and buys the Pelican Hotel in Miami, Florida.

1992
Diesel advertising begins to win international awards and Renzo Rosso buys a farm near the Diesel headquarters in Molvena, northern Italy.

1993
Renzo Rosso learns how to snowboard (taught by his sons) and is soon taking entire Diesel staff on weekend snowboarding expeditions.

1994
55-DSL sports line is created.

1995
Renzo Rosso reaches 40 and, to celebrate, publishes an enormous book—*FoRty*—about himself, his friends, and Diesel.

1996
Diesel flagship stores are opened in New York and London. First catwalk show, in New York.

1997
U.K. music/style magazine *Select* votes Renzo Rosso one of "The 100 Most Important People in the World." Style Lab "catwalk" show held in London. Diesel wins international advertising Grand Prix at Cannes for two commercials.

1998
Renzo Rosso named Advertiser of the Year at Cannes festival. The sixth Diesel store in the U.S. opens, in Santa Monica, California.

Index

Acknowledgments

The publishers wish to thank Renzo Rosso and all at Diesel for their kind assistance with all aspects of this book. Special thanks to Wilbert Das, Antonella Viero, and Alessio Cian Seren (Diesel Headquarters, Italy) and Wendy Brierley (Diesel UK).

Photographic credits
Lowe Howard Spink, London: page 17 right, 47 top right, 52.
Paradiset Agency, Stockholm: pages 12, 18, 24, 25, 29 right, 30 top and right, 31, 38, 41, 42, 45, 46, 47 (other than top right), 53, 59, 61 "Successful Living."
Guy Ryecart photography: pages 13, 14, 15, 26, 28, 29 left, 35.
All other photographs courtesy Diesel SPA